Student History Notebook of America

by
Maggie S. Hogan

Cover Design and Maps
by
Josh Wiggers

Graphic Lay Out and
Design
by
Cindy Wiggers

Published by GeoCreations Ltd.
Dover, DE

*Thanks to Celeste Rakes and Muriel Van Wave for their valuable input.
And special thanks to Tyler Hogan, Bob Hogan, Sarah McDowell, and
Michael Redmond for helping with the sample journal pages.*

To God be the glory ~

MSH

Student History Notebook of America

Printed in the United States of America
First Edition

To distribute this book contact:
GeoCreations, Ltd.
toll free (877) 492-7879

Dear Teachers/Parents,

Taking notes, writing essays, keeping journals, researching, and organizing thoughts are all nearly-lost methods of discovery and learning. By helping your students develop these important skills you're doing them a lifelong favor. They will become better learners and thinkers by acquiring these habits.

Do you develop your own history curriculum? This book can serve as a guide and as a repository for material covered. Kathryn Stout's book, *Guides to History Plus,* is an excellent companion book, providing comprehensive lists of questions, objectives, topics and resources by time periods, and more.

If you're using this book as a supplement to a prepared curriculum, you'll find it will help you organize your student's work as well as provide guidelines for hands-on learning not always included in traditional course work.

Before beginning, please peruse the entire book to gain an overview of what's included. Older students might benefit from reading this section, also. It's important to note that there are many suggestions, ideas, and samples on the following pages. Please choose what works best for you and leave the rest. There are more options here than one would reasonably expect to do in a year!

Tips:
1. Photocopy the timeline pages before beginning work on it in order to have extra pages, if needed, to tape in the book.

2. Use colorful jumbo paperclips to tab the sections your student will be using on a regular basis.

3. Consider cutting out (literally) the entire Introduction and any unused Appendices at the end of the year. Subsequently, The *Student History Notebook* would begin with your student's Table of Contents and would only include his or her work in it - nice for showing off!

4. Be cognizant of your student's ability and hold him only to reasonable expectations. Be an encourager!

I hope this book becomes a tool that make your job of educating simpler and more enjoyable.

Sincerely,

Maggie S. Hogan

Student History Notebook

How can we make history come alive for our students? By getting them intimately involved in their studies. Keeping a student notebook is a very effective method for pulling them into history discoveries. Writing down what they're learning from a variety of sources, organizing the information in a way that makes sense to them, and having some freedom to choose which rabbit trail they'd like to follow, all adds up to an increased sense of ownership and involvement on students' parts.

Keeping a notebook is a time-honored way to:
- Learn research skills
- Develop writing skills
- Improve orderly thinking skills
- Cultivate independent study habits
- Ignite a love for learning

This notebook is a way to organize efforts and develop a framework on which to build. Even though the notebook provides structure, it also allows plenty of opportunity for individual creative efforts.

Read through this introduction to gain an overview on how to most effectively use this approach. Then choose which sections of the notebook you wish to use and plan accordingly. Many will choose to use the entire notebook but others will decide to use only the components that best suit their needs. The *Student History Notebook* is a tool, not a rule! Considering your objectives and your student's needs and learning styles, create a plan of action that works best for you.

Younger students need involvement with the teacher. Older students not accustomed to working independently outside of workbooks/textbooks may initially need extra coaxing to get into the routine. All students benefit from having expectations and procedures thoroughly explained.

Important Tip:
Assign writing time each week. It doesn't work to tell them to write if you don't actually carve out writing time in your class schedule. Ideally, time will follow time spent in reading, research, and discussion.

Have students summarize what's been learned each week. Younger students may do so by narrating what they remember. Gently help them, over time, to narrate in an organized manner. Some students may prefer to dictate their summary. (As their writing skills improve, they'll be capable of doing more writing.) Other students may prefer to type their information, print it out, and tape it directly into the notebook. The "right" way is the way that best works for your student. The point is to get into the habit of developing the discipline to think through the information received, process it, and then to clearly explain what's been learned.

Consistency is important here. Consistency on your part will pay off dividends in consistency on the student's part. Teachers need to be consistent to:

- Provide time/space/materials
- Check on student progress
- Hold student to reasonable standards

Journal Pages
The Journal section comprises the bulk of The *Student History Notebook.* These pages can be used in a myriad of ways. On pages 17-18 are eight samples just to get you started!

Use the pages in a variety of ways or choose one or two formats that work best for your needs and assign that format to your student. Here are a few more ideas for ways in which to use the Journal pages:
1. Chronological note taking of each week's lesson
2. Summary of each time period or event covered
3. Diary approach - writing as if the student were in the story
4. Repository for meaningful items. Attach with tape:
   a. postcards
   b. pictures or drawings
   c. brochures
   d. ticket stubs
   e. maps
5. Recording data about significant people
6. Top lines may be used for quoting a primary source or relevant Bible verse
7. "State Study" using one state per page.
8. Writing important speeches or poems, possibly to memorize.
9. Boxes at the bottom are great for map, artwork, and diagrams

Looking Deeper
What is "Looking Deeper"? It's going beyond the initial reading of an event and trying to discover its whys and significance. Look for:

- Cause and effect
- Motivations
- People behind the story
- Common characteristics
- Relevancy to Scripture
- Significance to today

Educators can't cover everything, but sometimes in trying to important events are treated superficially. Keep in mind - the goal isn't to cover huge time periods as quickly as possible. Sometimes in-depth studies are called for; other times overviews are appropriate.

Textbooks tend to present pre-digested and pre-thought information. Active inquiry, thinking things through, comparing and contrasting views - that's where long-term learning happens!

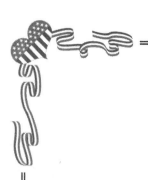

This isn't a "learn to regurgitate, fill-in-the-blank, take the test, get a grade and be done with it" method!

The *Student History Notebook* method emphasizes:
- Questions
- Curiosity
- Research
- Organization
- Processing
- Retention

Hands-On History

Although some people seem to absorb all they need to know from simply reading material, most of us benefit from hands-on approaches when possible. Decide how much of this you can realistically do. Planning ahead makes hands-on projects easier to implement. Competent students may help younger siblings with projects in a patient manner, thus benefitting everyone in the long run. For some, a project every week is a reasonable goal, for others that isn't realistic.

Summary:
- Be realistic regarding available time
- Utilize older student's talents
- Plan ahead
- Follow the plan

Project Ideas:
- Salt-dough maps, dioramas, shadow-boxes, costumes, models, etc.
- Cooking and serving food from particular times or ethnic groups.
- Music. Listening to or making music representative of a time or culture.
- Watching videos or plays (not technically 'hands-on,' but fun anyway).
- Games. Buy, borrow, or better yet, make your own games. Terrific learning tool.
- Computer Software. There are good ones out there. Beware of junk, though.
- Play acting events. (A homeschooled teen in Wilmington, DE, started his own Civil War re-enactment group made up of homeschooling kids and their families. They now participate in large scale re-enactments all over a tri-state area!)
- Field trips. Much easier when studying American history than ancient civilizations.
- Constructing/drawing timelines or posters or maps.

"Real People" Projects:

1. Interview older Americans and record their stories. Add them to your timeline. Make a picture album with information collected.

2. Interview 1st or 2nd generation immigrants. Record their story and the impact immigration had on them, and how in turn their culture has impacted America.

3. A genealogical search of your own family's history ups the interest factor for most students.

All these stories may inspire your student to further study and will be beneficial to everyone involved. A simple booklet might be a great way to finish the project. Videos or audiotapes of the subjects might also be appropriate.

History - What Do I Teach When?
There's no "official" standard for what history should be taught in which grade. It's not only different state-to-state but even from district-to-district. That's because there really isn't one "right" order.

This frees you to teach one time period to a variety of ages together. Older students require more detail and should explore cause and effect, motivations, and other abstract ideas. Younger students need more concrete information. And regardless of age, all will enjoy the exciting stories of real people and real events.

The older student's notebook will reflect his questions, research, ideas, and his conclusions. The younger student may have more of a "scrapbook" type notebook with drawings of wagon trains, a photo of his homemade johnnycake, and his hand-drawn map of the Oregon Trail.

Show children that history is a series of stories about people just like them. **Capture the stories and you'll capture their interest!**

Timelines

Children don't have an adult grasp of time. Sounds obvious, doesn't it? Then why do adults often teach as if they should understand it the same way? What does a young child think of when they hear, "A very long time ago"? He might think of something that happened last week, last year, or maybe even a few years ago. He probably isn't thinking decades or centuries!

Ruth Beechik, in her excellent book *You Can Teach Your Child Successfully* says this about timelines:
> *"For children, timelines are not for pulling together the scattered pieces of knowledge, as they do so well for adults; children haven't yet collected enough pieces to pull together. What time lines can do for children is to provide a framework into which they can put pieces of knowledge as they learn them. For this framework purpose, timelines should be very simple - so simple that children can memorize them."*

Here's one way to help demonstrate the stretch of time we call history. Stretch a clothesline across a large room, garage, or even out of doors on a nice day. Have students write important facts or questions about American history onto index cards. (They could range from "The year I was born," to "When did great granddad Luis came to America from Sicily?" to "Davy Crockett was born.") Once you have a range of questions or events, spend time helping students find dates for their cards. Decide how much time you want your timeline to cover. For example, are you beginning with the Vikings, Columbus, the Pilgrims or the Civil War? Once you know how many years you are covering you need to do a little math:

> Measure the timeline and convert to inches. Divide the inches by the number of centuries being spanned. For example:
> > Clothesline is 20' or 240"
> > Covering 1492 - 2001 = 509 years
> > 240 ÷ 5 = 48
> Now we have four feet per one hundred years.

Make century strips out of cardboard and have the students attach them in the appropriate places with clothespins. Next, add their index cards in the right places with clothespins.

To illustrate a broader view of time, point out that if we were to go back to the time of Christ, the clothesline would have to extend back an additional 60 feet!

This timeline can be made more elaborate by adding mementos about events and people to the timeline. A toy outdoorsman figure could symbolize Daniel Boone and the Wilderness Trail, a miniature Statue of Liberty could represent the waves of immigrants in the early 1900's, and a baby rattle might be the perfect thing to depict your student's birthday.

A simpler introduction to timelines can be accomplished by making one of your own family's history, beginning with the birth of the grandparents and ending today. Make it out of posterboard or make copies of the timeline included in this book.

Of course, as students mature, timelines can be done in more detail. With practice, they will begin to use them to pull together pieces of information they learn yearly.

When looking at timeline books or filled-in timelines, notice how time periods are labeled and dates are chosen. Each is different. Pick and choose the method you prefer or develop your own. Here are two examples of American history time periods. (This can be done any number of different ways.)

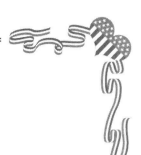

Time Periods

Example #1

1400's -1600's	Early Exploration
1600's - 1770's	Colonial Times
1760's - 1783	American Revolution
1783 - 1790's	Birth of a Nation
1800 - 1900	Westward Ho!
1820 - 1877	*Civil War and Reconstruction
1870's - 1900's	Industrial America
1918 - 1945	World Wars I and II
1946 - 1999	Post War and Modern America

Example # 2

1400's - 1620's	Exploration & Discovery
1605 - 1770's	Colonization
1750's - 1790's	Revolutionary Period
1775 - 1900's	Westward Expansion
1820 - 1865	A Nation Divided
1865 - 1900's	Reconstruction and Expansion
1850's - 1910	Rise of Industrial America
1914 - 1929	World War I and Roaring Twenties
1929 - 1945	Great Depression and World War II
1945 - 1989	Cold War
1946 - 1970	Post War and Turbulent 60's
1970 - 1999	Modern Day America

*Also referred to as the War Between the States, the War of Northern Aggression, and other names.

As you can see from just these two examples, American History can be divided in a number of ways using a variety of labels and dates. Why? Because history doesn't 'happen' in neat and orderly chunks of time!!

For other examples of time periods see Kathryn Stout's *Guides to History Plus,* Ruth Beechik's *You Can Teach Your Child Successfully*, and other resource books. The point behind the timeline labels is to give you and your student a framework upon which to build. Develop one that best suits your student's needs.

Because history doesn't happen in orderly chunks, you may find it simpler to follow themes rather than progressing in strict chronological sequence. Finish one theme through to a certain year in history, then backtrack and pick up another theme and follow it.

For example, when teaching about the Westward Expansion, one could begin with Daniel Boone and the Wilderness Trail in 1775. Include events from the Native American perspective (or do a whole separate unit on it).

Along the way one might also cover transportation (wagon trains, canals, pony express, and railroads - great fun!), the Gold Rush, The Homestead Act of 1862, and the immigration waves from 1830 - 1910.

Obviously, many other very important events happened between 1775 and 1910. The Civil War comes to mind. Perhaps it was touched on as you covered the Westward Expansion. But you'll want to focus on the events leading up to this war, followed by the war itself, and then the period of Reconstruction. That much material might be better organized as a separate unit.

Think of teaching history as a series of spirals. Follow along sequentially for awhile, but go back to pick up other important threads as necessary and take them forward.

History is messy! It's intertwined and can rarely be packaged neatly like a math curriculum. If you remember you're teaching about real people and real events you'll begin to find it easier to go with the flow of the story and not worry too much about "covering everything in the right order."

Filling out a large, colorful timeline as you go along will help illustrate events in the order they happened, even if you didn't study them in that sequence. For example, as you study the Civil War, add "South Fires on Ft. Sumter - Civil War Begins" at the same place you earlier recorded "First Pony Express." So even when you must go backward, just remember to add to the timeline.

Keep the timeline simple, colorful and fun!
In addition to one large timeline that everyone can see at a glance, it's worthwhile for students to construct their own student timeline. One is included in this notebook. If your student works better on a larger scale, it's certainly fine to do an oversized timeline. Student timelines may focus on:

- Events as they are learned (a general, chronological timeline)

- Specific themes (military, music, science inventions, etc.)

- Important people

- Detailed special interest

One student may continue working on his elaborate Civil War timeline even while the study has progressed into the next century! Another may prefer to follow the life of Benjamin Franklin. Encourage these deeper studies, even when you feel it's time to "move on." This is how hobbies develop which can benefit the student in many ways. Now they are experts on the Civil War or Ben Franklin!

Assignment Sheet

Optional. Tips for Using:

1. Assignments may be recorded directly onto this page when following pre-determined lesson plans.

2. Convenient for teachers and students who wish to stay organized and prefer for all their papers to be kept together in one place.

3. May also be used as a "goals" page. Information for the student to learn or memorize may be listed here. Record general assignments, "List the main events leading up to the American Revolution" or specific goals, "Memorize the presidents in order of their terms served."

Geography

Resources:

Historical Timeline Figures

The Ultimate Geography and Timeline Guide

Usborne Book of World History Dates

Scholastic's *Everything You Need to Know About American History*

World Almanac for Kids

Facts Plus Almanac

Kingfisher's *Illustrated History of the World*

DK *History of the World*

Rand McNally *Historical Atlas of America*

The Wall Chart of World History

Timetables of History

Instruct students in the use of geography reference tools before assigning them work in this subject. Many American youth today are not being taught geographic skills. If this isn't your strong subject (perhaps you had little or no training yourself), don't despair. Take this opportunity to learn right along with your student. *The Ultimate Geography and Timeline Guide* is highly recommended for teaching this critical, yet often neglected, subject.

The following outline maps are included for a wide range of American History mapping projects:

- USA with States Labeled
- USA Physical Features, Labeled
- USA
- USA Physical Features
- North America
- Atlantic Rim
- USA West of the Mississippi
- USA East of the Mississippi
- Make Your Own Maps (two blank pages for students to draw their own)

Issues to understand before giving geography assignments:

1. Choose appropriate reference material. Consider:
   a. ***Typeface.*** Look carefully at the font style and size. If it's too small for the student to read clearly, it will cause frustration. Younger students need bigger, clearer fonts. As atlases increase in complexity, the font size decreases. Conversely, older students may not be able to find needed information in a children's atlas.

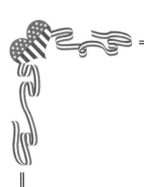

b. *Lay-out and design.* Busy and detailed maps that may appeal to a high school student may easily frustrate a fifth grader.

c. *Content.* Look for atlases containing material complimentary to your lesson plans. While studying American history, you'll be pleased to have a USA atlas on hand. (These too, come in a variety of levels.) If animal habitats are a part of your studies, look for an atlas that includes habitat maps. Some atlases are almost strictly maps, while others include a wealth of other infor mation: flags, planet and earth statistics, and cultural information.

d. *Atlas age*. Is your only household atlas a ponderous volume from college days? It may be useful for some projects, but its political maps will be hopelessly out of date. Good, useful atlases can be had for under twenty dollars. Invest in a new world atlas every few years, keeping it both current and age appropriate.

e. *Variety.* No single atlas is going to answer every question asked. One atlas may be strong in political maps, while another is a great atlas for thematic maps, and another has exciting, eye-catching cartography. Just as most of us have more than one Bible and dictionary, it makes sense to have more than one atlas. (Especially important if your students' are more than a few years apart in age.)

f. *The points above also apply to other reference materials.* Almanacs are available in a variety of styles to meet different needs. For about ten or twelve dollars you can buy a new children's almanac each year. If you're not accustomed to using one, you'll be amazed at the wealth of material available in almanacs. Take the time to browse through one and then teach your students how to use it. Adult almanacs contain more information but often the print is quite fine. Children's almanacs are more readable and often have a "Wow! Read me!" look.

g. *Wall maps.* Look for:
- Africa in the center so that Asia isn't split. (It's hard to explain why one continent appears on opposite sides of a map!!)
- Politically up-to-date.
- Pleasing to look at and read.
- Enough labeling to be helpful, but not cluttered.

h. *Globes*. Best for teaching:
- Topics such as: latitude, longitude, hemisphere, rotation, etc.
- Hands-on tool for physical geography concepts.
- Relationships between places.

Atlases
These Rand McNally atlases are good general references:

•*Classroom Atlas*: Elementary

•*Answer Atlas*: Jr High

•*Premier World Atlas*: Jr. high and up

•*Goode's World Atlas*: high school and up

Tip: Since globes become outdated quickly, buy an inexpensive one widely available at department stores during back-to-school sales.

2. Teach students which reference to use when:

    a. ***Road Map*** - for specific driving directions.

    b. ***Wall Map*** - countries and continents at a glance. Excellent for current events and the "big picture." Not well suited for detailed map work.

    c. ***Globe*** - countries and continents in relationship with one another. Excellent for physical geography/science topics such as: latitude, longitude, hemisphere, rotation, eclipses, seasons, day and night, time zones, etc. Not well suited for most "find this place" type activities.

    d. ***Atlas*** - for finding specific places, political and physical features, and thematic information such as climate maps, population maps, etc. Not well suited for the "big picture" of physical relationship of continents/countries around the world.

    e. ***Almanac*** - concise information in one easy source on a huge variety of topics. Typically updated yearly. (Think of it as the "highlights" of an encyclopedia.) Not well suited for in-depth studies.

    f. ***Encyclopedia*** - in-depth information on countries, peoples, places, events, etc. Not well suited to current events - only as current as its publishing date.

    g. ***Dictionary*** - concise definition, pronunciation, and spelling of geographic terms. What is a "butte" and how do you say that?! Understand each reference's strengths and weaknesses to pick the right one for the job.

Non-essential, but often helpful, are good computer programs that would supplement many of the above categories. Read reviews and talk to people before you buy, because there is plenty of junky "edutainment" software available.

Questions

Beginning on page 92 is a section labeled "Questions." We're all naturally curious. Unfortunately, that curiosity is all too often dulled by an unimaginative education. Students who are habituated to the "teachers ask questions and I fill in the answers" type of schooling may lose interest. Answering questions may be seen as an end, rather than a beginning. Students who've already become burned out may find that asking and answering their own questions is a novel, and possibly intimidating, idea. Students work when they are truly interested in something. The search becomes relevant when they have a stake in it. Interest is gener-

ated and enthusiasm builds. This doesn't happen overnight, though. It takes patience and guidance from an involved adult.

Initially, it might work well for the teacher to write down several questions each week that may lead the student into areas of particularly interesting reading. This acts as a springboard, increasing interest in the subject. The student can add his own questions which arose during his reading.

Tips on Getting Started:
1. Pick a period of history, gather a few (not all!) good books on the subject - preferably those that are well-written, colorful, and appealing.

2. Browse with the students, enthusiastically. Act as secretary, writing down their comments and questions.

3. Choose a few of their questions. Ask them to be detectives or historians and search for answers. (Initially, try to pick questions for which you think they'll be able to find the answers.)

4. Students then record their questions in this notebook on the "Questions" pages.

5. Provide them with a trip to the library, access to an expert, or your own reference materials to begin their sleuthing.

6. Teach them to "skim" and how to use the index in a book to determine its suitability for answering their question.

Tips for Using the "Questions" pages:
1. Student records questions of interest. (May then write answers directly into the Journal pages.)

2. Or, the teacher records questions in the notebook for the student to research.

3. Use a combination of the above techniques.

The Value of "Why?"!
Your students will notice there are often conflicting opinions, "facts," and answers to many questions. Discuss why this is so and how to best discern answers. Points to consider:
1. Writer's or historian's biases or prejudices
2. Poor or incomplete records
3. Distance from the event (time and/or location)
4. Lack of perspective
5. Misunderstandings/poor communication
6. Sinful motivations (pride, greed, etc.)
7. Other reasons?

How might we discern what is true?
1. Prayer
2. Wisdom gained from maturity/experience
3. Checking sources:
      a. trustworthiness/reputation of source
      b. proximity to event (time/location)
      c. verification by other sources
      d. perspective - looking back on event
4. What other methods might we use?

Help students judge the worthiness of an opinion, which sources to trust or mistrust, how to look for bias in reporting, etc. It's important they know that just because something is in print, doesn't mean it's true. Who said it, what's their reputation, and do other reputable people substantiate what was said?

Primary Sources
Getting information from a primary source at least gets you back to first hand, often eye-witness accounts. Of course, primary sources were still written by fallible human beings writing from their own, often limited, perspective.

Internet
Internet information can be truly amazing or truly awful. It's especially important to be discerning here. Consider the web site or source carefully. Look for:

- Credentials
- Motives
- Trustworthiness
- Verification

The old adage, "You can't believe everything you read" is even more applicable concerning information posted on the web!

Appendix Pages
Look it Up - Write it Down - Remember it!

Tips for using the Appendix Pages:
1. Topics for further research
2. Topics to memorize
3. Extra credit or additional studies

The Appendix Pages include:
• **Vocabulary**

• **Scriptures and Quotes**

• **Resources and References**

• **Presidents**
List the presidents in the order of their term(s) served. (Putting the presidents in order makes a good secondary timeline.)

• **States and Capitals**
States and Capitals may be written several different ways: according to geographic regions, alphabetically, chronologically.

• **Preamble to the Constitution**
Followed by blank lines on which the student may copy this important document.

• **The Pledge of Allegiance to the Flag** (also provided for copying)

• **Our Government Today**
A form to fill out and keep handy. Gather pertinent information about contacting elected representatives.

• **Star Spangled Banner**
Lyrics to the first and fourth stanzas of the "Star Spangled Banner" are included. Useful for memorizing.

• **Currency and Coins**
This form for money provides a springboard for a unique look at history. Who's on them? What symbols are used and why?

• **Fifty U.S.A. Quarters**
Here's a place to record information about the 50 states while collecting each of the 50 state quarters as they are released.

• **Book List**

• **Field Trips and Projects**

Sample Journal Pages

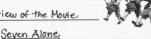

Review of the Movie

<u>Seven Alone</u>

Seven Alone is based on the book, On to Oregon by Honore Morrow. The book was based on the true story of the Sager family who left their home in Missouri in 1843 for the Willamette Valley in Oregon. Along the way both parents died, leaving the eldest child, John, in charge of his six younger siblings. It was an exciting movie and it showed the hardships and life on a wagon train. I was amazed at how these children survived. Watch John change from an immature, lazy brother to

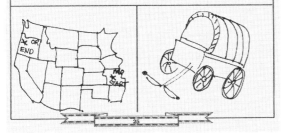

Native Americans

And Where They Lived

There were many different Native American tribes spread across North America when the English settlers arrived. Many of the first arrivals to this new country made friends with natives, including the Pilgrims, French fur trappers and traders. Missionaries like George Whitefield, David Brainerd, and others befriended these people. But, there were many conflicts, too. Settlers didn't understand the cultures, language and customs of the

North and NE Tribes
Algonquin   Southeast
Conestoga   Catawba
Delaware   Cherokee
Iroquois   Chickasaw
Mohawk   Creek
Seneca   Natchez
Winnebago   Shawnee
               Tutelo

A traditional Navajo home called a "Hogan" made of tree branches and mud

---

The Story of the
<u>Star-Spangled Banner</u>   ★

When we visited the Smithsonian Institution in Washington, D.C. we saw the original flag we call the "Star-Spangled Banner." It's huge! No wonder Mr. Key was able to see it waving over Ft. McHenry that morning. Have you ever heard the story of the "Star-Spangled Banner"? It happened like this:

In 1812, hostilities between America and Great Britain developed into a full-fledged war. (Even though it lasted several years, we call it the War of 1812.)

The Star-Spangled Banner:
* was sewn in 1813 by Mary Pickersgill
* was 30' x 42'
* used about 400 yds of bunting
* had 15 stripes
* had 15 stars } represented the 15 states
* (each star was 2' tip to tip)
* became the national anthem on March 3, 1931.

Attack on Pearl Harbor
America Enters the War

At 7:00 a.m. Sunday, December 7, 1941 radars at the base on Pearl Harbor in Hawaii picked up a large number of approaching aircraft. Thinking they were American planes, an alarm was not sounded. From about 7:55 a.m. until 9:00 a.m. over 300 Japanese aircraft attacked. They destroyed hundreds of American aircraft, sunk or damaged 18 warships, and killed over 3,700 people, including civilians.

I asked my grandparents about Pearl Harbor. They remember hearing the news very clearly. My grandmother, newly married to a Navy ensign, was coming home from evening church

ISLAND OF OAHU   PACIFIC
                                       OCEAN

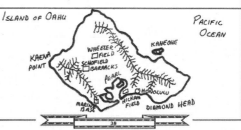

KAENA POINT   WHEELER FIELD   KANEOHE
              SCHOFIELD BARRACKS
              PEARL
              HONOLULU
MARINE BASE   HICKAM FIELD   DIAMOND HEAD

Sample Journal Pages

The Battle of Antietam Creek

by Tyler Hagan

Two officers from the Union Army, Corp. Mitchell and Sgt. Bloss, were marching. When they sat down to rest, Corp. Mitchell found a piece of paper wrapped around some cigars. He motioned Sgt. Bloss to look at it. Corp. Mitchell was excited about the cigars while Sgt. Bloss noticed the paper had writing on it. What a discovery! It was General Robert E. Lee's military plan for the Confederate army!

Using this information, the Union army found the Confederates and ordered an attack. The Confederates defended themselves well, but many men were lost on both sides. The Union tried to

Fact File
Name: The Battle of Antietam Creek
Date: Sept. 17, 1862
Duration: 1 day
Location: Sunken Road and Antietam
          Creek in Maryland
Commanding Officers:
    Union: Maj. Gen. George McClellan
    Confederate: Gen. Robert E. Lee
Dead/Wounded/Missing: 22,000!

X = UNION FORCES
□ = CONF. FORCES

"My mother was the making of me. She let me follow my bent." T. Edison

Thomas Alva Edison was an energetic and mischievous boy. He asked so many questions his teacher thought he was a problem child. But "Al's" mother knew he was very bright, and he learned better by doing things. She began to homeschool him. He set up a lab in their basement and happily experimented there until he was twelve. Then he began to work fulltime for the railroad. This job had many exciting moments, like when he accidently set the baggage car on fire with his experiment! This first

Thomas Edison's Timeline	1,093 patents! Most in History!
1847 Born in Milan, Ohio	vote recording machine
1859 went to work for railroad	Phonograph
1863 worked as night telegraph op	electric locomotive
1868 1st real invention: vote rec.	1st motion picture device
1871 Married 1st wife (she died)	alkaline storage battery
1876 built lab in Menlo Park, NJ	quadruplex telegraph
1877 first Phonograph	many more!
1931 Died at age 84	

Corn Bread

A recipe from the Old South

A long time ago, corn was very important. People in the south used it in many dishes like corn bread, corn pudding, hush puppies, and for feeding the animals. Slaves used it a lot, too. We made it in a cast iron skillet, like people did then. We baked it at 400° for about 22 minutes. It was very good.

Ingredients:
1 C sifted flour
1 C sifted cornmeal
1 T baking powder
½ t salt
1 T sugar
1 egg
1 C milk
¼ C oil or lard

Directions:
Sift first 5 ingred.
Beat eggs with milk + oil.
Make a little hole in dry
  ingred. and pour egg in.
Stir until blended.
Pour into greased 8 x 8 x 2 pan.

Bake 400° 22 minutes.
Yum!

Field Trip Notes
Fort Clatsop: Lewis + Clark

Our family went on a trip to Ft. Clatsop in Oregon. After reaching the Pacific Ocean this is where Lewis and Clark built a fort to stay in during the winter. It was a very interesting place but much smaller than I had imagined. It's hard to believe about 33 people stayed there. It's only 50' x 50' with two parallel rows of cabins connected by palisades and gates. Walking in the same rooms that these brave men once lived in was exciting. At the museum there, I learned

6 Major Accomplishments:
① Made it to the Pacific + back.
② Described 122 animals new to science
③ Described 178 plants new to science
④ Brought back vocabulary, cust. of tribal populations, + details of culture 40+ tribes.
⑤ Formed positive relations w/ many of these tribes.
⑥ Discovered NA much larger than thought!

Student History Notebook of America
Table of Contents

Student

Year

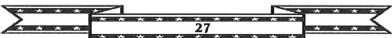

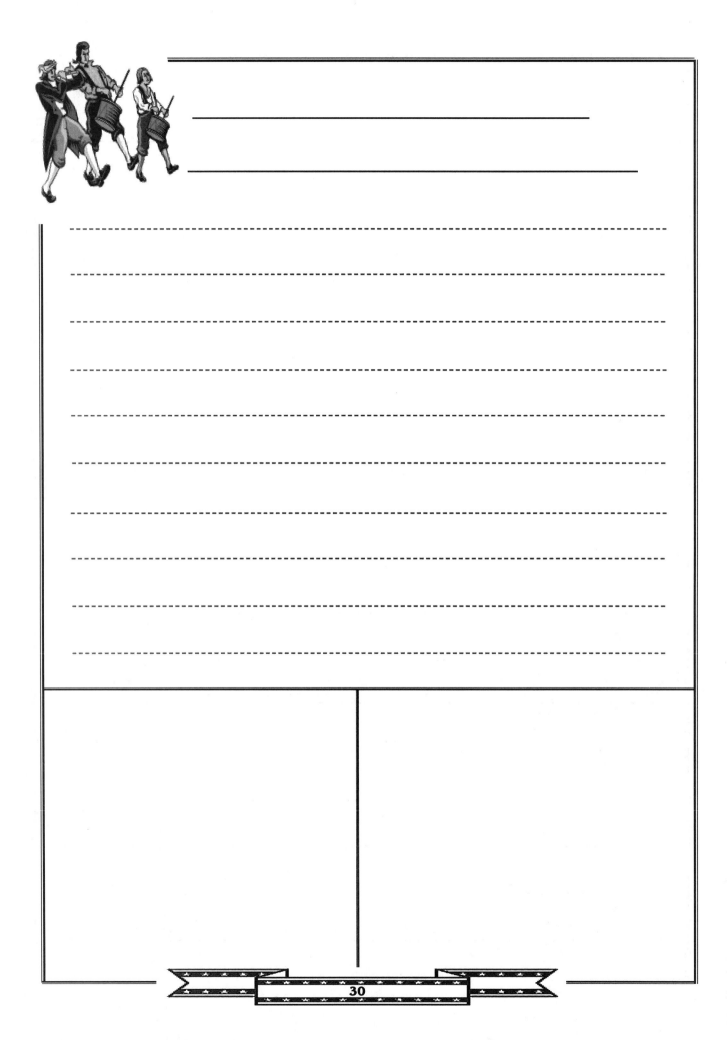

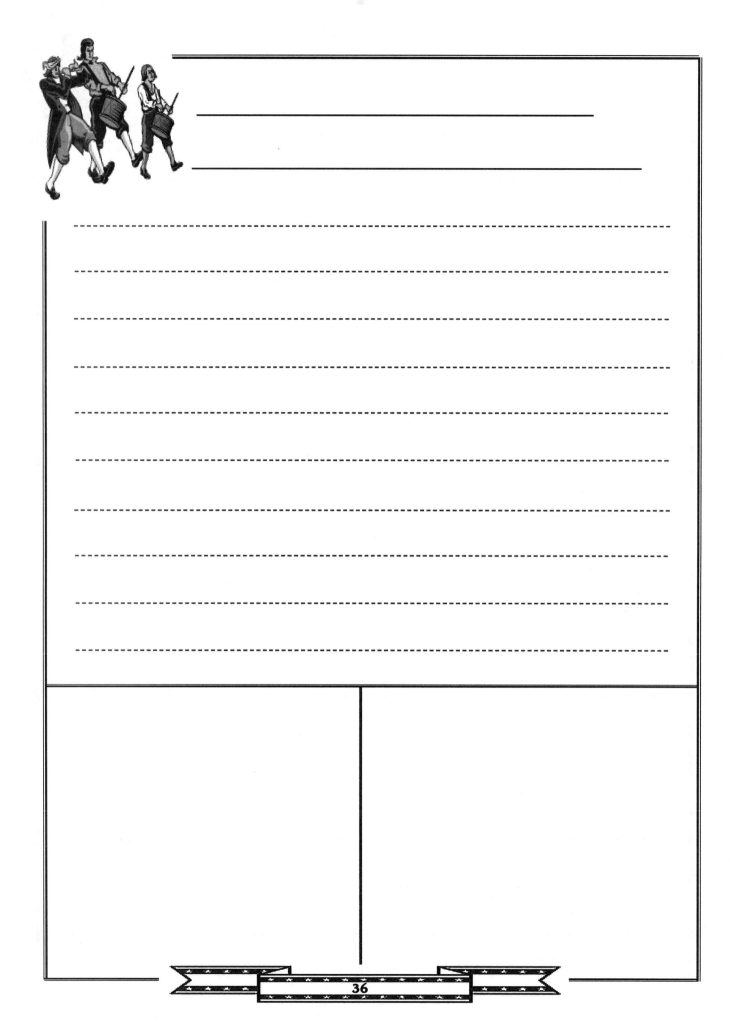

Summary

Summary

Assignment Log

Date   ✔

Assignment Log

Date   ✔

Date	Assignment	✔

Map Work Log

Places	✔	Physical Features	✔
		Routes/Movement	

Directions

Label places on your map in black, capital in red, bodies of water blue, mountains brown, and other physical features in green. Use various colors for shading in regions or tracking movements/routes (i.e. the Transcontinental Railroad or the Oregon Trail.) Place a check mark (or the day's date) next to an item you've added to your outline map.

Map Work Log

Places	✔	Physical Features	✔
		Routes/Movement	

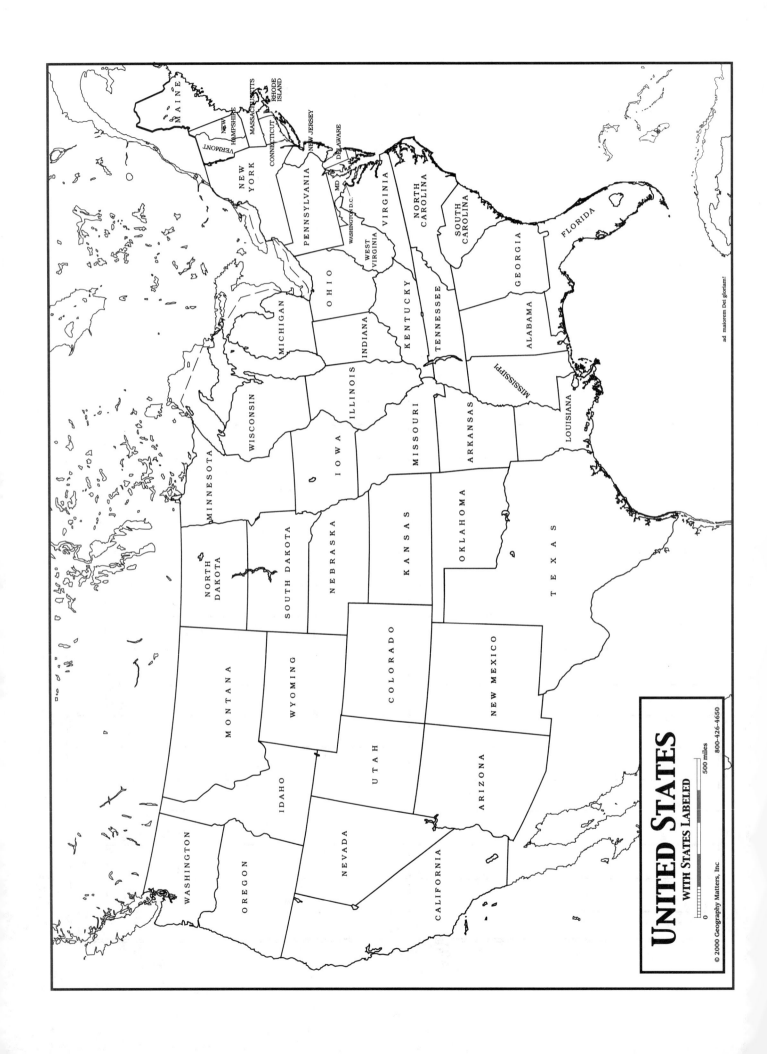

UNITED STATES
WITH STATES LABELED

500 miles

0

800-426-4650

© 2000 Geography Matters, Inc

ad maiorem Dei gloriam!

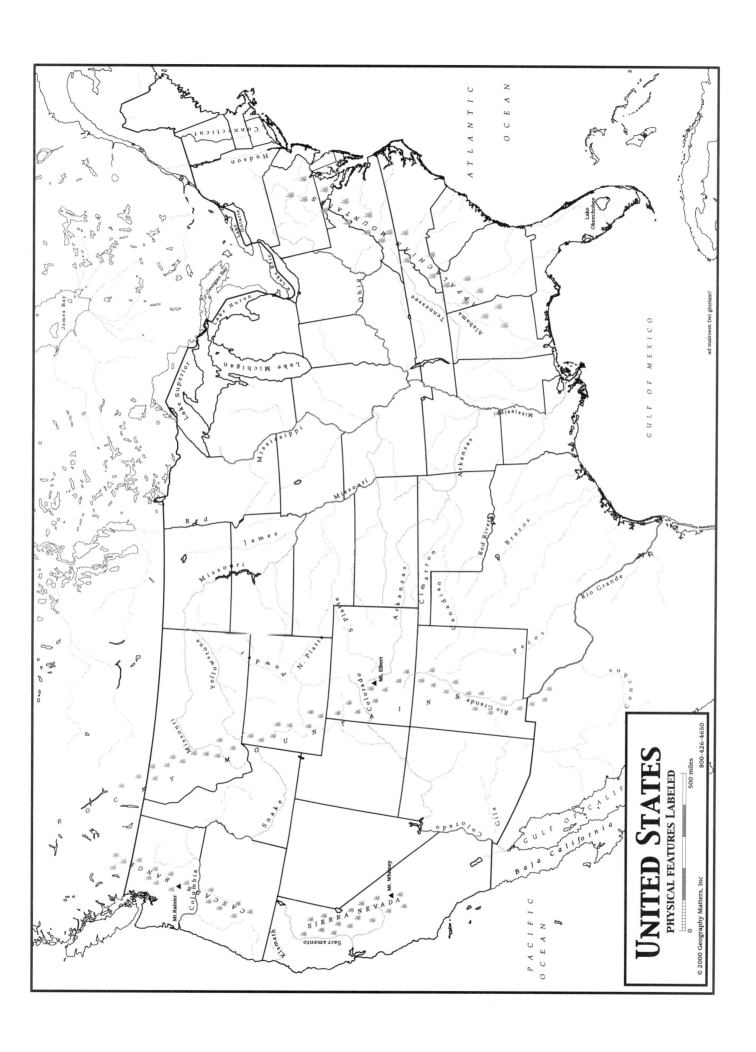

UNITED STATES
PHYSICAL FEATURES LABELED

© 2000 Geography Matters, Inc

800-426-4650

0   500 miles

ad mairoem Dei gloriam!

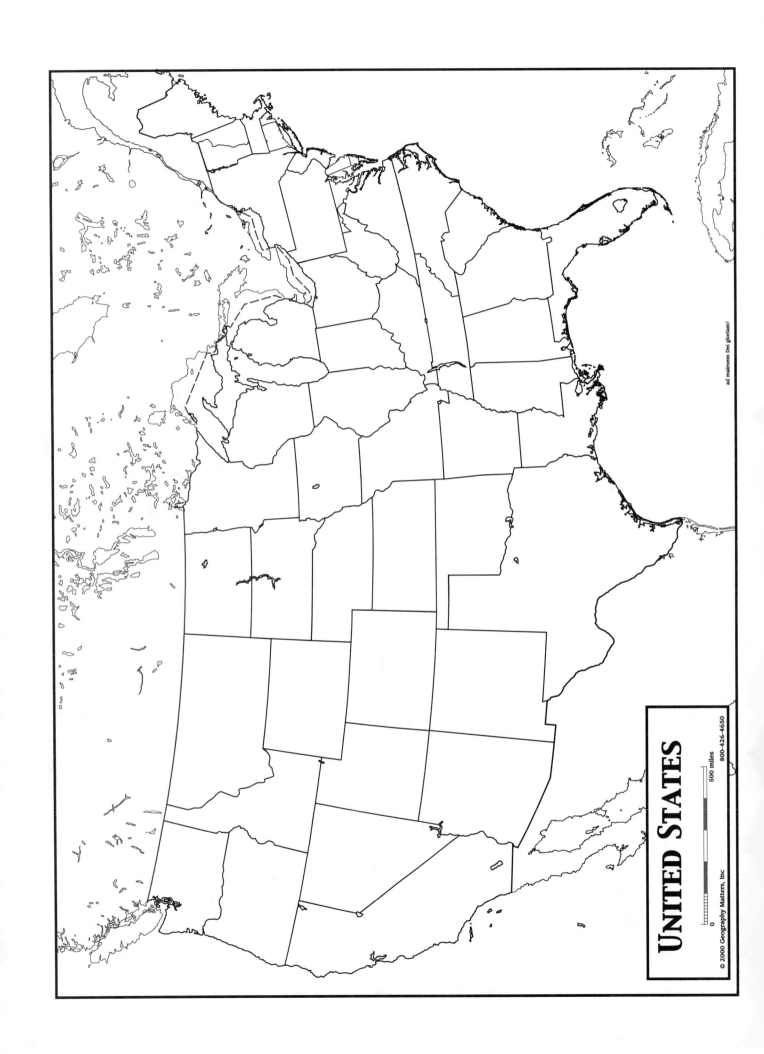

UNITED STATES

500 miles

0

© 2000 Geography Matters, Inc.

800-426-4650

ad maiorem Dei gloriam!

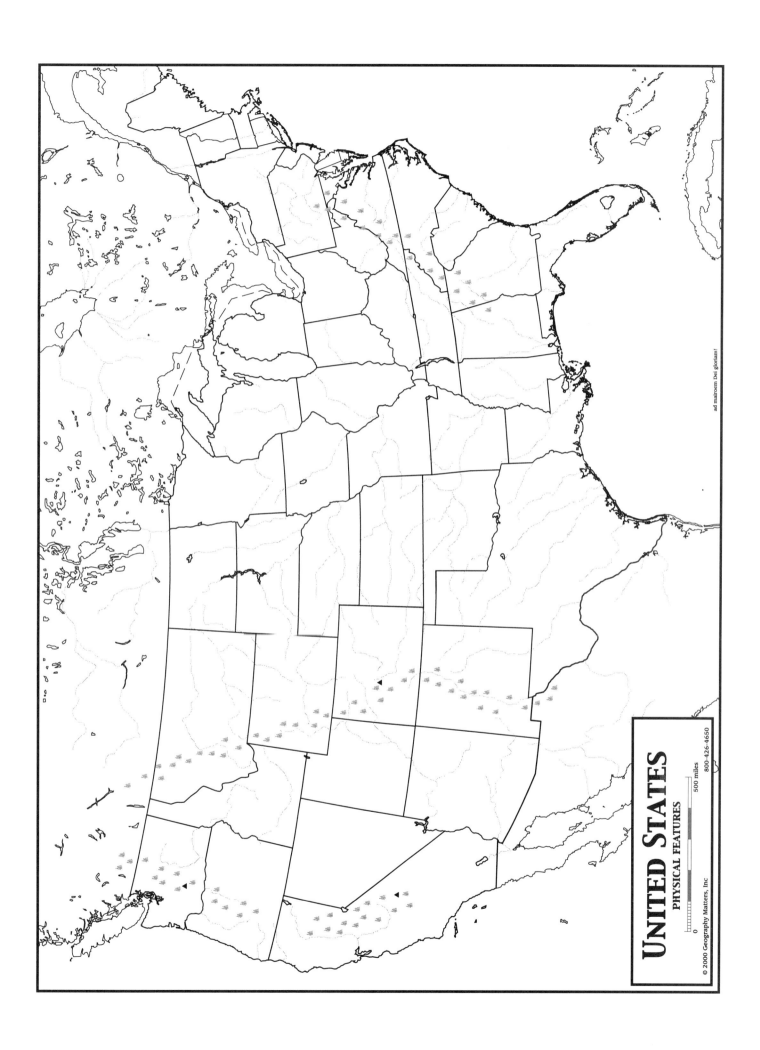

UNITED STATES

PHYSICAL FEATURES

0   500 miles

800-426-4650

ad maiorem Dei gloriam!

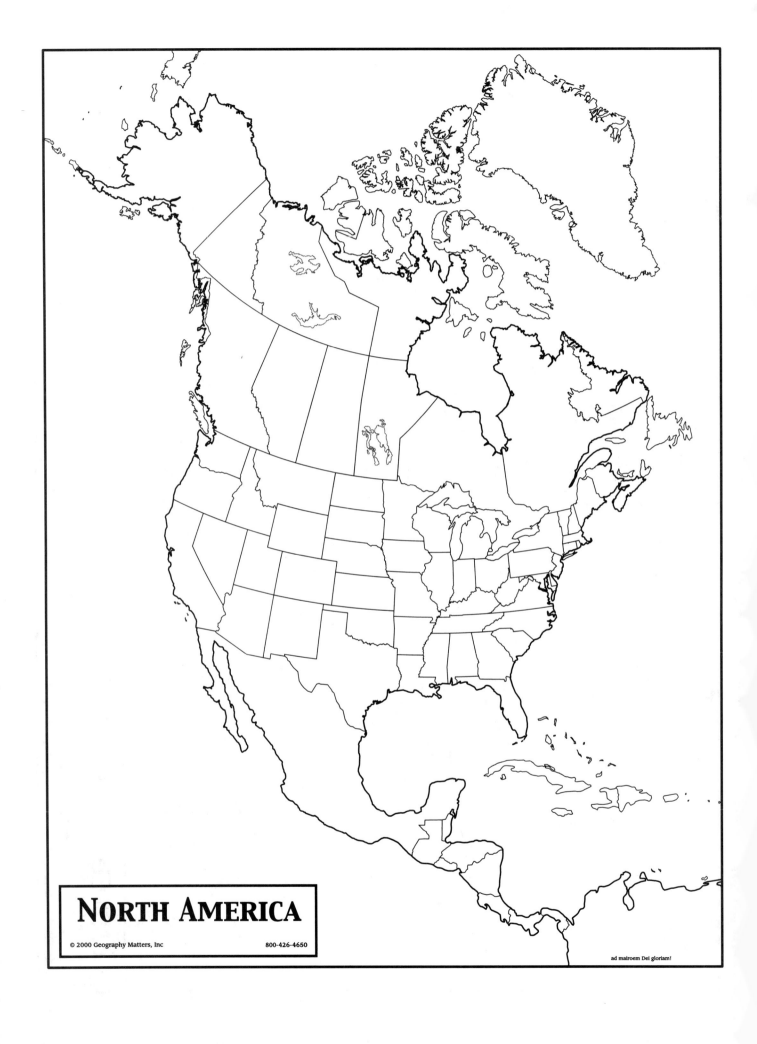

NORTH AMERICA

© 2000 Geography Matters, Inc   800-426-4650

ad maiorem Dei gloriam!

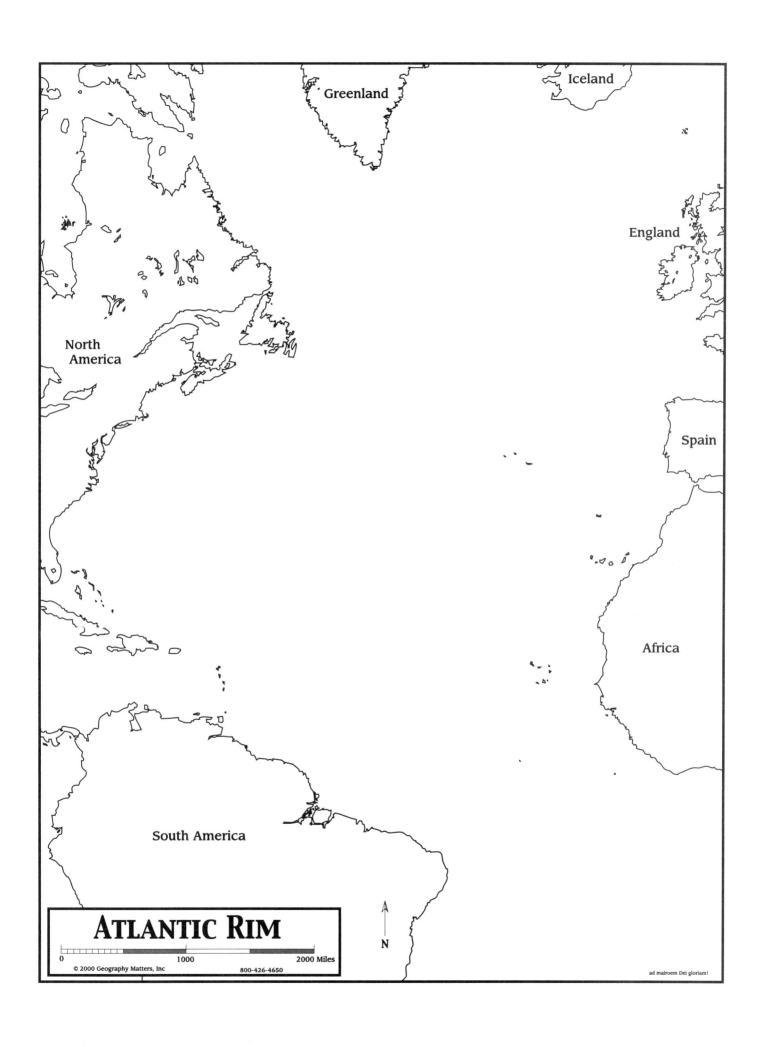

Iceland

Greenland

England

Spain

North
America

Africa

South America

ATLANTIC RIM

0   1000   2000 Miles

© 2000 Geography Matters, Inc

800-426-4650

N

ad mairoem Dei gloriam!

UNITED STATES
WEST OF THE MISSISSIPPI

0 |||||||||||||||||||||||| 500

© 2000 Geography Matters, Inc   800-426-4650

ad mairoem Dei gloriam!

UNITED STATES
EAST OF THE MISSISSIPPI

0   500 Miles

© 2000 Geography Matters, Inc   800-426-4650

ad mairoem Dei gloriam!

KEY

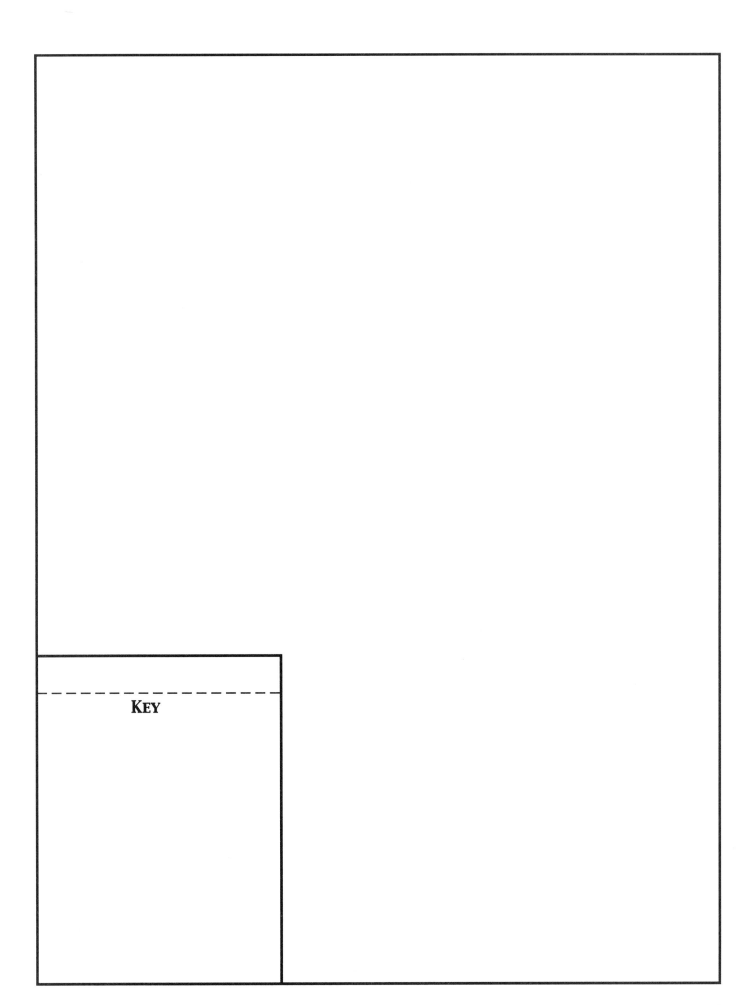

KEY

Timeline Log

Date	Person/Event	Interesting Facts	✔

Color-code your timeline. Here are some suggestions. Europe (blue), USA (red), Science (green)

Timeline Log

Date	Person/Event	Interesting Facts	✔

Color-code your timeline. Here are some suggestions. Europe (blue), USA (red), Science (green)

Timeline of American History

Timeline of American History

Timeline of American History

Timeline of American History

Questions

Questions

Vocabulary

Word	Definition	✔

Vocabulary

Word	Definition	✓

Quotes and Scriptures

Resources and References

USA Presidents

Name	Interesting Facts	Term
1.		
2.		
3.		
4.		
5.		
6.		
7.		
8.		
9.		
10.		
11.		
12.		
13.		
14.		
15.		
16.		
17.		
18.		
19.		
20.		
21.		
22.		

USA Presidents

Name	Interesting Facts	Term
23.		
24.		
25.		
26.		
27.		
28.		
29.		
30.		
31.		
32.		
33.		
34.		
35.		
36.		
37.		
38.		
39.		
40.		
41.		
42.		
43.		
44.		

States and Capitals

Ab.	State Name	Capital City		

Ab.: Place two letter state abbreviation in this column.

100

States and Capitals

Ab.	State Name	Capital City		

Ab.: Place two letter state abbreviation in this column.

States and Capitals

Ab.	State Name	Capital City		

Ab.: Place two letter state abbreviation in this column.

States and Capitals

Ab.	State Name	Capital City		

Districts and US Territories

The Preamble to the Constitution of the United States

We the people of the United States, in order to form a more perfect union, establish justice, insure domestic tranquility, provide for the common defense, promote the general welfare, and secure the blessings of liberty to ourselves and our posterity, do ordain and establish the Constitution for the United States of America.

Copy the preamble here in your neatest handwriting:

For a scholarly yet useable reference to the Constitution, see *The Factual Guide to the Constitution for the United States of America*, by RJ Smith. Available from:

    The Eureka Group
    7672 Montgomery Road
    Cincinnati, Ohio 45356
    $25.00 plus shipping

These two great resources on the constitiution are published by Christian Liberty Press:

The Land of Fair Play
The Story of the Constitution

The Pledge of Allegiance

I pledge allegiance to the flag of the United States of America and to the Republic for which it stands, one Nation under God, indivisible, with Liberty and Justice for all.

Copy it here in your neatest handwriting:

| |
| |
| |
| |
| |
| |
| |

What is the proper protocol when reciting the Pledge of Allegiance?

What is the proper protocol for taking care of a United States Flag?

Contact your **State Senator** for information on obtaining at cost, US flags that have been flown over the US Capitol. They are available in a variety of sizes from approximately $7.50 and up.

Star-Spangled Banner

by Francis Scott Key, September 1814

O! say, can you see, by the dawn's early light,
What so proudly we hailed at the twilight's last gleaming:
Whose broad stripes and bright stars through the perlious fight,
O'er the rampart as we watched were so gallantly streaming?
And the rockets red glare, the bombs bursting in air,
Gave proof through the night that our flag was still there:
O! say, does that Star-spangled Banner still wave
O'er the land of the free and the home of the brave?

What was happening while Mr. Key penned these words?

How many verses are there?

Here are the lyrics to verse four:

O' thus be it ever when free men shall stand
Between their loved homes and the foe's desolation;
Bless'd with victory and peace, may our Heaven-rescued land
Praise the Power that hath made and preserved us a nation,
Then conquer we must, for our cause it is just-
And this be our motto - "In God is our trust!"
And the Star-spangled Banner in triumph shall wave,
O'er the land of the free and the home of the brave.

American Symbols

The Great Seal of the United States	*The Bald Eagle*	*The Liberty Bell*

Motto: In God We Trust (Officially adopted July 30, 1956)

106

Our Government Today

Nationally Elected Officials

Official Phone Number	Address
President	
Vice President	

Local and State Elected Officials

The year in which I'll be able to vote:_____

107

Currency and Coins

$	Paper Person and Symbol / Building	¢	Coin Person and Symbol / Building
1.00		.01	
2.00		.05	
5.00		.10	
10.00		.25	
20.00		.50	
50.00		1.00	
100.00			
500.00			

Fifty USA Quarters

Released in Order of Statehood

State	Design/Symbol	State	Design/Symbol

Book List

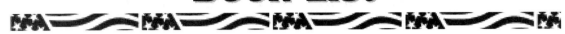

Title	Author	Type	Date

Types: F Fiction   NF Non-Fiction   H Historical Fiction   A Autobiography
B Biography   R Reference   M Magazine/Newspaper

Field Trips and Projects

Date	Objective	Result

RECOMMENDED BY THE AUTHOR

Uncle Josh's Outline Map Book

Outline maps are a foundational part of teaching geography and history. Here are 100+ maps to use year after year, regardless of topic or time studied. If you like using the maps in *The Ultimate Guide* you'll love adding this broad assortment of maps to your library of outline maps! Includes each of the fifty states, all seven continents, ancient historical regions, important war arenas and more! Rivers are lightly shaded and surrounding borders are left intact. You've got the whole world covered in this one-of-a-kind book! Reproducible, 112 pages. ($19.95)

LARGE-SCALE OUTLINE MAPS
Great for studying Continents, Ancient History, and More!

Continents Map Set

Includes (approx.) 17" x 22" maps of Africa, Europe, North America, South America, 23" x 34" 3A Map (Asia/Australia/Antarctica double-sided map), PLUS bonus USA map. ($16.95 paper, $34.95 laminated)

Ancient/Bible History Map Set

Includes (approx.) 17" x 22" maps of Europe and the Middle East, Israel and Eastern Mediterranean (double-sided), Ancient Civilizations PLUS bonus Timeline of History. ($9.95 paper, $24.95 laminated)

Hands-On Geography

Packed full of multi-grade, inexpensive (often free), activities and resources with reproducibles. Make homemade books, games and notebooks that can be used to study any people, country or locale. Written for home schooling by home schoolers this book has clear instructions, including age level appropriateness, approximate preparation time and activity time, and materials needed for each activity. A valuable resource that makes geography more fun to learn and teach. Recommended for K-4, 112 pages. ($15.00)

The Scientist's Apprentice

A one-year science curriculum that is understandable and exciting for K-6th grade students. Experiments, games, crafts, recipes, writing, and songs teach to different learning styles. Reinforces orderly thinking skills. Reproducible pages and easy-to-follow directions make this a practical program families will love. More interesting than a text book and easier than a unit study. We've done all the work for you! ($26.95)

The Ultimate Geography and Timeline Guide

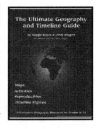

The Reader's Choice Award winning Ultimate Geography and Timeline Guide is a non-consumable, "all-you-need-to-know" curriculum for teaching students from kindergarten through high school. Entertainingly written and thoughtfully laid out, this book is sure to become a favorite geography resource. Excellent for both those who enjoy developing their own curriculum as well as those who like complete ready-to-use lesson plans.

The Ultimate Guide helps teachers:

- Make learning geography fun using the outline maps, hands on activities, and games included.
- Choose geography materials and supplies.
- Teach geography with historical novels using *Hans Brinker or the Silver Skates*.
- Select maps and use assignments provided for U.S. history studies.
- Improve student's history comprehension by using a timeline.
- Develop geography/science units with volcano and weather units .
- Select great Internet sites on geography, history and science.

The Ultimate Geography and Timeline Guide, 353 Pages, K-12, $34.95

Mark-It Timeline of History

Students record historical events on the timeline to gain a broader perspective of history and to enhance memory retention. Two and one half inches between lines provide ample space for depicting overlapping events. Side one is marked with dates, side two is undated for any in-depth study. Laminated, durable, and reusable when using water-based (Vis-a-Vis) pens. Use as poster or cut in strips to stretch out for 21 feet of history! 23" x 34" ($9.95)

Historical Timeline Figures

Printed on quality, colored card stock these figures are coded with icons and computer generated graphics to aid student memory retention: seven borders reflect historical eras; twelve icons represent topics; five colors show where the event occurred. Generic and Family Heritage Figures allow for creating and customizing your own figures. Includes two games to aid memory and test knowledge. These same figures are included in the Ultimate Geography and Timeline Guide. ($25.00)

To order any of these resources or for full catalogs contact:

Geography Matters, Inc.
P.O. Box 92
Nancy, KY 42544
(800) 426-4650
geomatters@geomatters.com
www.geomatters.com

Bright Ideas Press
P.O. Box 192
Magnolia, DE 19962
Toll free (877) 492-8081
info@brightideaspress.com
www.brightideaspress.com